New Lobbies & Waiting Rooms

New Lobbies & Waiting Rooms

Daniela Santos Quartino

COLLINS DESIGN

An Imprint of HarperCollins*Publishers*

NEW LOBBIES AND WAITING ROOMS
Copyright © 2008 COLLINS DESIGN and LOFT Publications

First Edition

First published in 2008 by:
Collins Design
An Imprint of HarperCollins*Publishers*
10 East 53rd Street
New York, NY 10022
Tel.: (212) 207-7000
Fax: (212) 207-7654
collinsdesign@harpercollins.com
www.harpercollins.com

Distributed throughout the world by:
HarperCollins*Publishers*
10 East 53rd Street
New York, NY 10022
Fax: (212) 207-7654

Packaged by:
LOFT Publications
Via Laietana, 32, 4.° Of. 92
08003 Barcelona, Spain
Tel.: +34 932 688 088
Fax: +34 932 687 073
loft@loftpublications.com
www.loftpublications.com

Editor and texts:
Daniela Santos Quartino

Editorial coordination:
Catherine Collin

Translation:
Lydia de Jorge

Art director:
Mireia Casanovas Soley

Cover:
Claudia Martínez Alonso

Layout:
Anabel Naranjo

Library of Congress Control Number: 2007943319

ISBN: 978-0-06-137486-9

Printed in China
First Printing, 2008

INDEX

6

INTRODUCTION

Beyond the physical area one encounters immediately after walking through the door of a building, the lobby is the decisive concept in the presentation of the space it is a part of. The success of the architectural launching will depend on the signals it transmits to its visitors.

Just like those people that inspire love, the lobby must generate that special chemistry that provokes the need for a deeper knowledge of the rest of the structure. Hence, the emphasis placed by both architects and interior designers for the appearance of the entry zones.

Contemporary vestibules are not, therefore, simple pathways that lead to the elevators and stairwells. In addition to displaying an attractive aspect, they are presented as flexible spaces that allow a great variety of activities. They are meeting points where one can see or be seen, relaxation zones, conversation areas, presentation settings, information points, and of course, waiting areas.

This is why they expand beyond traditional limits, acquire new shapes and coexist with other spaces in a sort of architectural crossbreeding.

Technology emerges as a new component of these enclosures, and in some cases imposes itself as the central element. Such is the case of the IAC lobby, designed by Frank Gehry and presented in this book together with those of other known architects and contemporary studies, the likes of Zaha Hadid, Massimiliano Fuksas, OMA, UNSudio, Peter Marino, Legorreta & Legorreta and Alsop Designs, just to name a few, or the waiting rooms created by designers like Ron Arad and Konstantin Grcic.

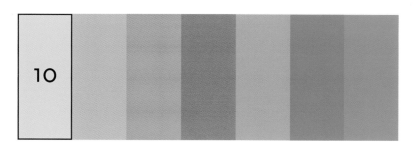

WATCH

Spectacular waiting rooms conceived to indulge the senses unconditionally.

© Luuk Kramer

AGORA THEATRE

UN STUDIO

Lelystad, The Netherlands | 2007

The building that houses the Agora Theatre has been conceived as a sculptural form that is made evident in the interior by means of its imposing lobby. It's a great open space, free of columns, that runs through the three stories of the building. It is situated in the center of the space, as is the main staircase that unites the two auditoriums, the dressing rooms, and the restaurants.

The vivid color of the stair's banister draws a line in the space that goes up in a zigzag and ends in a skylight. The warm tones that are predominant in this space combine with the yellows and oranges of the outside of the building and are inspired by photographs of the sunsets in Lelystad.

The lights in both the *foyer* and the corridors of the theatre, change colors as the time for the start of the shows gets near, culminating in a bright yellow that invites the audience into the auditorium.

GEEN TOEGANG

RLET ZAAL ONEVEN

RLET ZAAL BALKON
RIGE ZALEN

SCARLET ZAAL ONEVEN

As the time for the show to begin draws near, the lights begin to change.

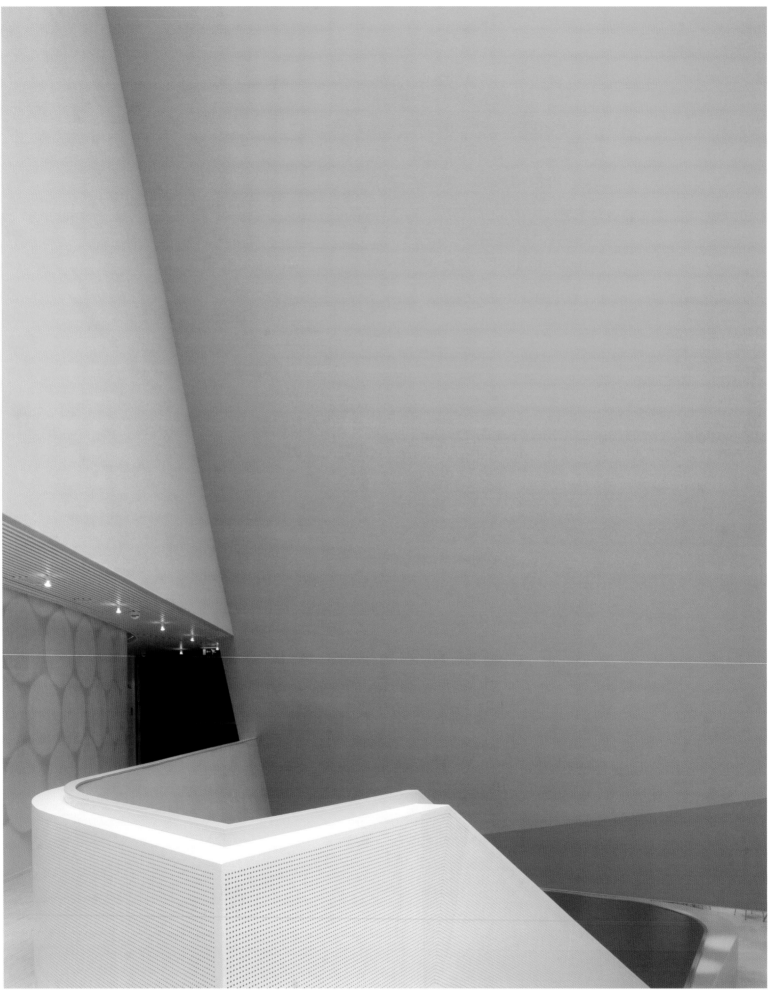

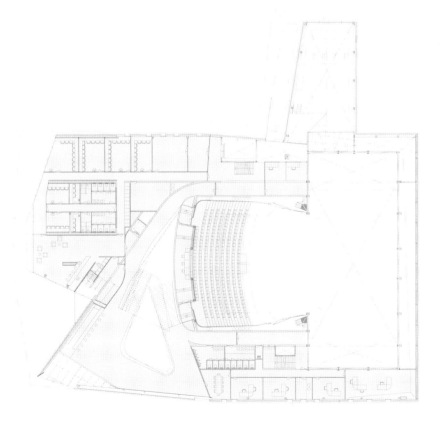

The central lobby is three stories high and intercommunicates through a zigzag-shaped staircase.

COPENHAGEN OPERA

HENNING LARSEN ARCHITECTS

Copenhagen, Denmark | 2005

Situated on Dock Island, on the opposite end of the Royal Palace, the Opera building opens to the sea through its glass front and allows glimpses of the impressive space that connects the auditorium with the great platform covered by a projecting 105-foot front ceiling.

From the outside, through the curved glass façade, the four-story lobby, crossed by horizontal steel bands, can be seen. A series of bridges connect to the auditorium, which is called "The Seashell" and that appears to float in the foyer. The exterior walls are covered with warm treated wood to resemble string instruments.

The sculptural lamps that are suspended at different heights and are made of delicate pieces of assembled glass, are the work of the artist Olafur Eliasson. The Opera House has a total area of 441,320 square feet, of which the lobby and auditorium occupy 75,341 square feet.

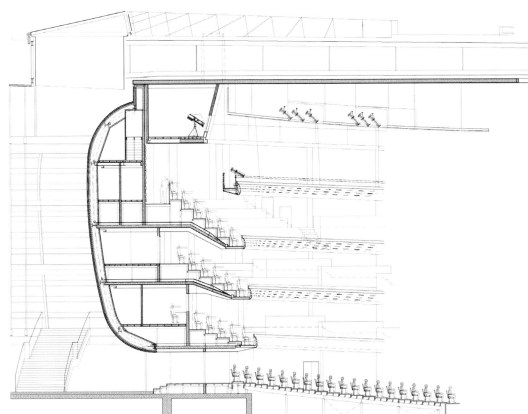

At night, the Opera House resembles a
lighthouse on the harbor, thanks to its glass-and-
steel façade that reflects the lights from the lobby.

The catwalks connect with the auditorium known as The
Seashell.

NETHERLANDS INSTITUTE FOR SOUND AND VISION

NEUTELINGS RIEDIJK ARCHITECTEN

Hilversum, The Netherlands | 2006

The grand lobby of the building that houses all of the Dutch audiovisual production since the early days of radio and television is the meeting place of the five structures that make up the entity. That is: archives and shops, museum, offices, reception for clients, and services.

The entrance leads to a sort of great trench with one of the walls made of inverted terraces, through which subterranean archive plants can be seen. The ample central space distributes the natural light that comes in through the skylights and the walls made of 2,100 colored crystals that make up the external skin of the building. The glass panels are digitally embossed with reproductions of 748 images from the archives of Dutch television's history.

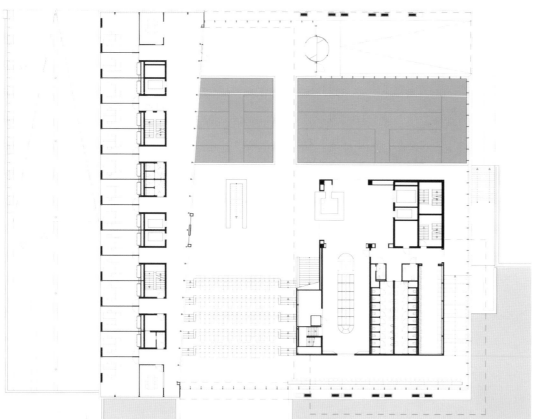

A deep trench allows the passing of natural light from the lobby to the subterranean area of the archives. The glass panels are digitally embossed with reproductions of images from the archives of Dutch television.

© Thomas Mayer

NORVEG COAST CULTURAL CENTER

GUDMUNDUR JONSSON ARKITEKTKONTOR

Rørvik, Norway | 2005

Corresponding to the long fishing tradition of the region of Rørvik, to the west of Norway, this exhibition center stands like a monumental sailboat alongside the coast, about to sail out to sea. The design is structured as three sails that represent tradition, supported by a body that makes reference to modern ships.

Parts of the sails cover the foyer of the building in a way that simulates a feeling of sailing. Inspired by the proportions of sailboats, the architect left a space between the floor and the mast of barely 4.6 feet. This forces visitors to sit and relax if they want to enjoy the magnificent view of the ocean.

The reception counter, on the other hand, simulates the bow of a ship and points toward the fiords; meanwhile, on the ceiling, special lamps called "acoustic seagulls" evoke seascapes.

The sails that cover the lobby invite the observing of the sea as if one were on board a ship.

The wood of the floors and the lamps that evoke
seagulls, complete the marine atmosphere of
the lobby.

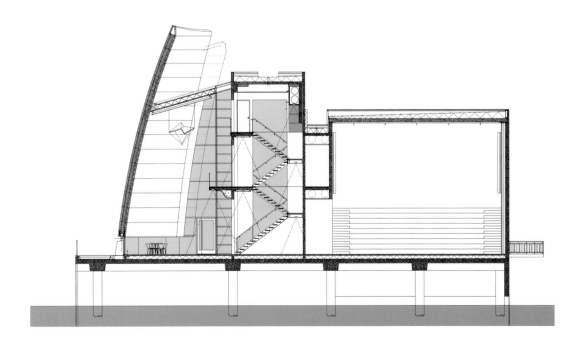

© Jorge Fabián Castillo

CASA DA MÚSICA

OFFICE FOR METROPOLITAN ARCHITECTURE (OMA)

Porto, Portugal | 2004

From the exterior, the Music House building looks like a cement polyhedron; a solid mass that rises above the side of Porto's historic zone. Once inside, a continuous route of staircases and platforms connects all the public areas and adjacent spaces of the two auditoriums.

The entrance, a space different from traditional lobbies, transmits an extraordinary dynamism. Upon entering the building, the visitor faces an ample and tall space with stairs that leads to the top levels.

The angular volumes of concrete, cut through the air and some of the visible pieces of the structure protrude though the walls. When going up on the aluminum stairs, sofas of intense colors distributed along the way, define the waiting areas that are distributed throughout the building.

Angular volumes of concrete, glass and metal
configure a surreal scenario.

The sofas in the waiting areas and the glass provide intense color to this solid building where cement predominates.

A series of spaces, sequences and staircases negotiate their
way around the auditorium.

Format
mediateca del trentino

FORMAT

BALDESSARI E BALDESSARI

Trento, Italy | 2007

Admired by movie stars, the likes of Marcello Mastroianni, Sophia Loren and Giulietta Masina, the lobby of this multimedia library situated in the center of Trento and its university district, is an inspirational encounter spot for movie lovers.

The strong geographic character of this space, with its black-and-white contrasts, evokes the classic era of the movies and frames the long and spacious lobby that runs from the entrance to the very heart of the library. A long information counter stands out, illuminated by an intense white light that reflects on the black resin floor.

The composition of the entrance hall is complete with glass walls illuminated from behind, and serves as support for interchangeable images. This gallery pays homage to the great icons of Italian movies.

Images project over the glass walls in a permanent homage to the great stars of Italian movies.

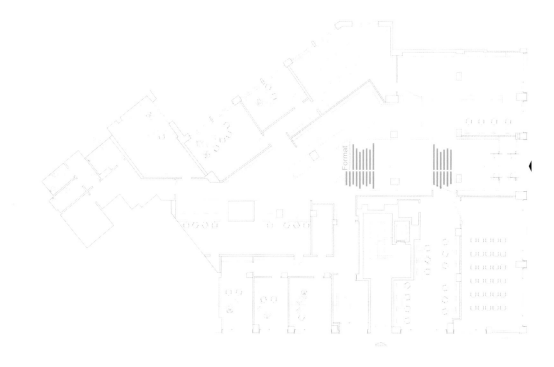

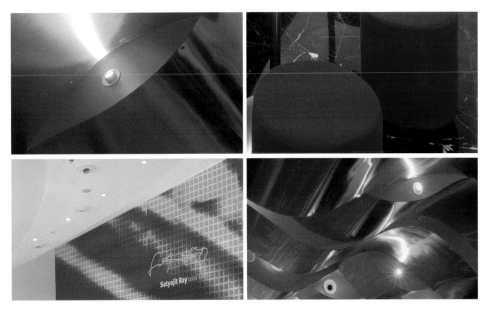

PVR MULTIPLEX JUHU

JESTICO & WHILES

Bombay, India | 2006

Located in the epicenter of the Bollywood industry, this stimulating and sensual foyer presents a scene intimately bound to the spirit of Bombay (currently Mumbai), the city where the most movies are produced in the world. In this space that conspires with fiction, the different shades of pink tie together the furniture in the waiting zones and the coffee lounge, whereas the coverings with Italian marble on the floor and walls provide light and a touch of glamour.

The undulating steel shingles on part of the roof of the foyer generate a volume that floats and dissolves the conventional limits between walls and the rest of the surfaces. The great, custom-made images situated in different areas of the foyer, reproduce scenes and characters from movies, as a tribute to the film heritage of the city where this platform lies, for the enjoyment of the seventh art.

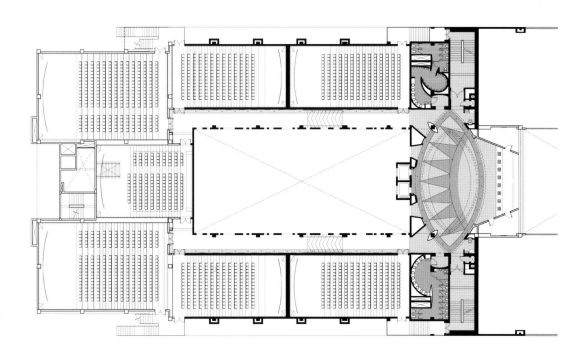

The undulating steel shingles dissolve the natural limits between the ceiling and the walls.

The Italian marble covering of the floor reflects the warm colors of the lobby and generates a vibrant atmosphere.

TRADE

Scenes that introduce a world-of-economy transaction, exchange of goods
and flow of capital funds.

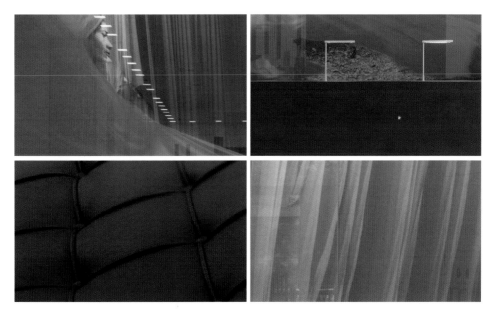

© Chris Gascoigne

6 DEVONSHIRE SQUARE

FLETCHER PRIEST ARCHITECTS

London, United Kingdom | 2006

Devonshire Square was constructed as a group of warehouses for the East India Company, in a zone that during the 1970s was the scene of an urban development plan in the city of London.

The renovation work of the building complex includes the individual design of each of the five reception areas. The new faces of these spaces are inspired by images of the products stored in the warehouses. This way, silk and other textiles, spices and other porcelains come to life in the greatly expressive murals of the reception.

This visual reference generates vibrant lobbies in which the bountiful influence of the East India Company in the construction and development of the city of London is irrefutably present.

The grand murals generate vibrant spaces that are reminiscent of the products stored in the warehouses of these historical buildings.

LOUIS VUITTON NAGOYA

CARBONDALE ARCHITECTS

Nagoya, Japan | 2007

An impressive sculptural structure at the entrance of this Louis Vuitton shop runs across the different levels of the building through an opening that is 36 feet in height. It is a cylindrical mezzanine made up of 6,000 aluminum flowers plated with polished steel, that appear to rain down from a luminous cloud. The interior of the cloud is lined with a warm layer of wood on which pieces of luggage, accessories and clothing are displayed.

As a means of tying the interior design to the façade that is composed of thousands of metallic strips that form a corkscrew, two spiral staircases intertwined like a double propeller have been installed; but true to the drawings of M.C. Escher, they never touch. Together, they look like a DNA chain that runs through the cloud of the mezzanine that connects the three levels of the shop.

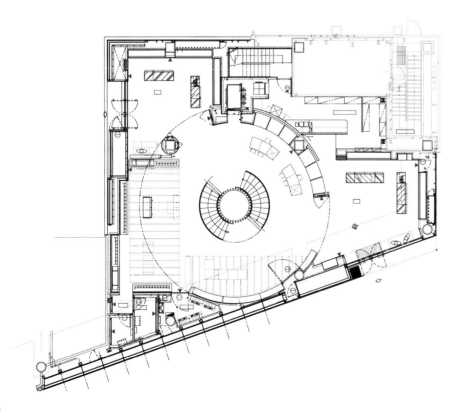

The thousands of aluminum flowers that outline the brand emblem appear to fall from the ceiling and attract visitors to the center of the shop.

The sculptural shape of the "cloud" in the lobby contrasts with the geometry of the rest of the premises.

© Vincent Knapp

CHANEL OFFICES GINZA

PETER MARINO

Tokyo, Japan | 2004

Situated on the top part of a ten-story building that houses one of the most impressive Chanel stores, the lobby and waiting area of the brand's executive offices present a beauty that's faithful to the style of Coco, the founder of this luxury firm.

The classic black-and-white contrast immortalized in pearls and black magnolias, idolized by Coco, is reflected in the interior architecture. These shades are present on floors and walls of bright and pure marble that alternate in different areas. Also, the framework of the glass dividers that separate the different spaces and the dressing rooms from the windows, inevitably evoke the black lines present in the most classic designs of the firm.

The furniture, minimalist and of strict geometric shapes, like the sofas, faces the street from the waiting area. The subtle metallic mesh that is seen from the inside reveals the design of the exterior façade, conceived as an abstract version of the classic Chanel tweed.

The furniture as well as the lining of the surfaces recall the style of Coco Chanel.

© Jurgen Landes, Roland Halbe

HOUSE WITHIN A HOUSE

BEHNISCH ARCHITEKTEN

Hamburg, Germany | 2006

The Börsenhalle, the classic headquarters of the stock market in Hamburg, needed to expand their offices to house spaces dedicated to conference rooms and waiting rooms. The architects solved this by creating a contemporary style structure in the ample hall, without pushing aside the character of the building that dates back to 1814. This way, they created "a house within a house" (Haus im Haus), made mainly of steel, glass and aluminum panels with LED lights. In the interior of the new structure, a grid of glass panels makes up the floor, allowing the light to go through the whole volume and generate a transparency effect. The ceiling, on the other hand, is made of rectangular screens of LED lamps, computer-controlled to imitate daylight.

The new space houses offices, meeting rooms, a social club, dining rooms, and a showroom to exhibit treasures from the Chamber of Commerce. A bridge on the second level connects to the ancient building, while the terrace offers impressive views of the exterior.

The traditional furniture in an absolutely contemporary context reaffirms the union between old and new that commands the "Haus im Haus" design.

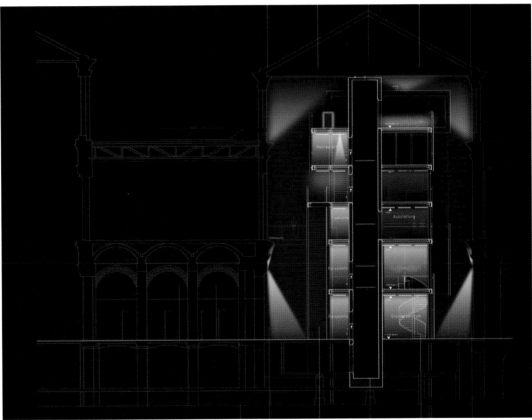

The two rows of arched windows over the first level provide generous natural light to the old structure and the new one.

© Beat Marugg/Infinite Light, Pedro Pegenaute

SABADELL BANK

MAP ARCHITECTS

Sabadell, Spain | 2006

Constructed in the 1950s, the building of the main offices of the Sabadell Bank has been submitted to a remodeling that looks to recover an image that is unified, contemporary, and recognizable as the institution's. The challenge for the architects has been the complex combination of historic conservation with a functional and technical updating.

The entrance is composed of a combination of floodgates that establishes a complex relationship between interior and exterior, but according to the premise of the project, guarantees the most transparency possible. The minimalist and abstract design chosen favors this condition.

Immediately adjacent, the operations patio, very luminous and white, dominates the offices. Its expressiveness is found in its limits defined by warm walls of dark wood on one side and cold steel on the other, that impose their presence in this harmonious space.

The entrance, made up of various compartments, has been redesigned to allow the most transparency possible.

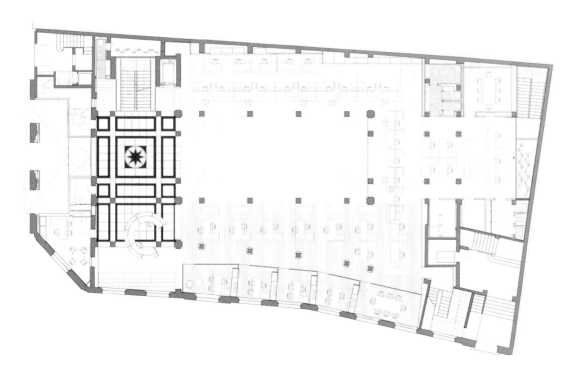

The metallic surfaces of the displays reproduce
the elegant designs of the marble floors.

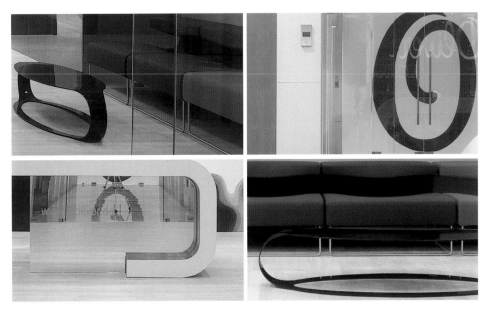

S. OLIVER OFFICES AND SHOWROOM

STUDIO 63 ARCHITECTURE & DESIGN

Hong Kong, China | 2006

As part of a German company with branches in every main city of the world, the architects considered it important to emphasize the geographic location of the office when it comes to its aesthetic definition.

This led to the idea of considerably enlarging a map of the city of Hong Kong and takes it to three-dimensions, until it became an almost abstract, colorful design. Located on the main wall of the entrance, the image dominates the reception area and provides character to this space of flat surfaces and minimalist equipment. According to the distribution of the offices, different colors and materials distinguish the function of each area. For each of the receptions a palette of reds and browns was selected and applied to the methacrylate walls, the sofas, and the lacquered tables of Chinese inspiration.

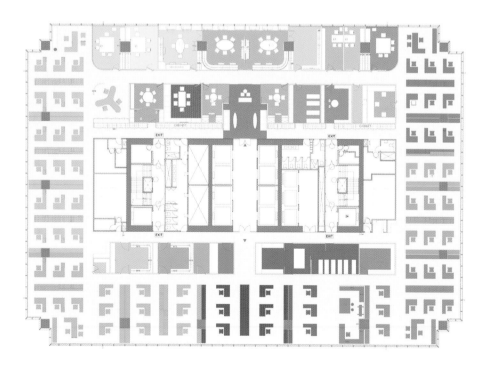

The abstract figure on the back wall is a simplification of a map of the city of Hong Kong.

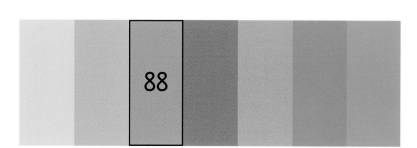

WORK

Working space whose anterooms have been designed to transmit
the identity of the corporations.

INTERACTIVECORP (IAC)

GEHRY PARTNERS

New York, United States | 2007

The new offices of the IAC Company rise like a crystal ship with undulating sails on the island of Manhattan. Its transparent walls allow a peek from the exterior of the spacious lobby where the main characters are a pair of giant video screens and spectacular lighting.

The largest screen, located in the West section, projects images inspired by IAC brands. This way, for example, Ticketmaster is promoted through geographic representations of all the places around the world where great concerts are taking place; whereas, Ask.com transmits headline news.

The smallest screen, located behind the reception counter, shows the locations of IAC offices throughout the world and provides information about the company. When the screens are turned off, an illumination system comes on and colors the space, giving it a diaphanous warm character.

The screen behind the counter is sensitive to touch and allows
visitors to rotate the representation of the Earth with their
hands and access the company's statistics.

The only existing furniture is the counter and a bench that
winds in front of a mural.

The bereft lobby comes to life and acquires content thanks to the video screens that project images related to the IAC Company.

The west-wall screen is the world's largest high-resolution video wall.

The video screens' colors can easily be seen from the outside, thanks to the building's glass skin.

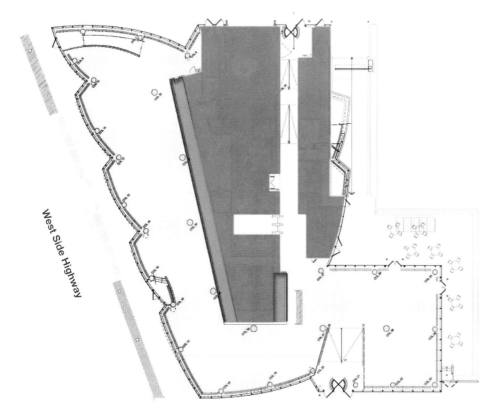

West Side Highway

© Frank Oudeman

MOMENTUM ST. LOUIS

THE LAWRENCE GROUP, NEW YORK

Missouri, United States | 2006

Upon entering this advertising agency's lobby, the senses recognize the stimuli caused by bold shapes and colors. Everything that can be seen symbolizes originality, freshness and novelty, and definitively, these are the concepts that an organization of these characteristics wish to convey.

The floor acts as a grand mirror that reflects the floating surface that covers part of the walls and ceiling. The marble reception floor is divided into strips with variable widths and colors that harmonize with the adjoining structures.

This sort of red carpet is visible from all the central areas of the agency, unifying the experiences of visitors with those of employees. It is a centralizing element that communicates the agency's main spaces from the reception and the waiting room areas to the central staircase, the offices and meeting rooms' areas.

The color stripes in the marble floor pass
through the reception and lead to the counter.

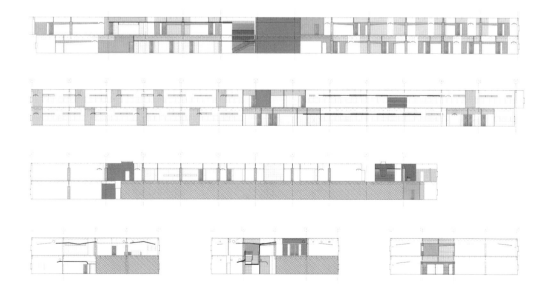

Bold colors and novel shapes honor the creativity that characterizes the advertising agency.

LEND LEASE EUROPEAN HEADQUARTERS

FLETCHER PRIEST ARCHITECTS

London, United Kingdom | 2006

The entrance to this building, located in the heart of London, is a great space completely visible from the exterior, which serves as a reception/meeting area, and exhibit zone. In accordance with the principles of development that sustain the environment promoted by the contracting company, the concrete structure has been left exposed. This not only contributes to the passive conditioning of the environment, it makes it evident that an old building is being recycled. On the great video screen installed in the area of the foyer, that can be seen from the outside, the company's activities are announced. On other occasions it is used for presentations. Of contemporary style, materials that are not harmful to the environment have been used in the interior, demonstrating that sustainability can be elegant and sophisticated.

The video screen in the reception area can be seen clearly from the exterior of the building. The coverings of one of the walls, plated in bamboo and cork, provide a warm touch to the concrete structure.

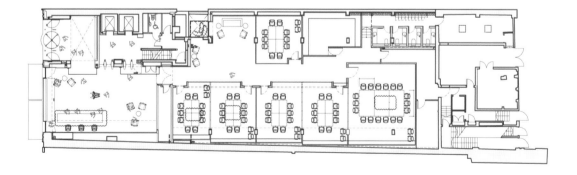

© Andre Morin

VAL-DE-MARNE DEVELOPMENT AGENCY

HERAULT ARNOD ARCHITECTES

Ivry-sur-Seine, France | 2004

How can a common block of offices be transformed, in record time, into an original, warm space, open to future modifications? The answer to this challenge is presented in simple principles of high visual impact.

Because it's a fairly new company that will continue to change in the upcoming years, everything has been arranged in a manner that facilitates new configurations of the space, such as hanging panels and the rolling flowerpots in the reception area. The line of cacti situated in the lobby announces to visitors that they are entering a zone of non-conventional work. The magenta curtain in the back emphasizes the impact.

The ceiling and the door that connect to the meeting room are made up of white-metal panels that alternate with long strips of colors, some of which present points of light in their interior that create an attractive geometry.

This lobby is a flexible area that hosts a variety of activities in the office.

The impacting contrast between the cacti and the
curtain at the back provides great personality to
this simple lobby.

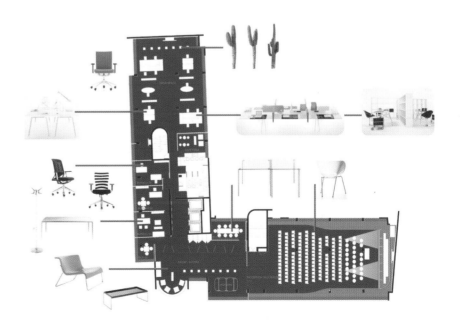

© Angela Auckland

CONSTITUTIONAL COURT

OMM DESIGN WORKSHOP

Johannesburg, South Africa | 2003

Located on the grounds where an old prison used to stand, today the building of the Constitutional Court of South Africa represents the values of democracy, and there is no better way to show it than with an ample foyer that also serves as a setting for the Chambers' public debates.

In South African society, the shade of a tree is a place of meetings, whether it be in schools, community meetings, or a simple social exchange. Thus the idea for this lobby, inspired by Sandile Goje's print "Making Democracy Work." The artwork represents a community with its elders, reunited at a table under a tree. A television camera that transmits the events to the outside world is filming the reunion. The central idea is that important things don't require monumentality.

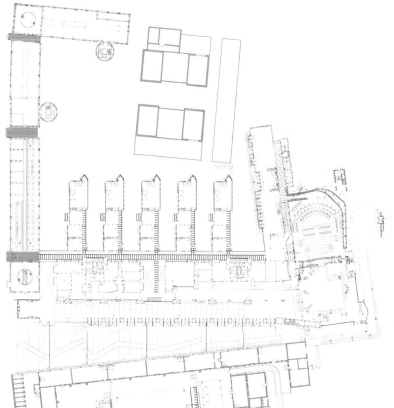

The hanging sculptures shaped like the branches
of a tree refer back to an old South African
tradition.

© Pez Hejduk

SPACE FURNITURE

HOLODECK ARCHITECTS

Vienna, Austria | 2006

What used to be an apartment that was provisionally used as an office for seven people, has been transformed into a spacious work zone with capacity for twenty employees. As a connecting element of the vast surface, a structure that adapts its function as needed has been designed.

Beginning with a waiting room on one of its sides, the composition transforms into a table, a bookcase, a support for a small garden and shelves to store files, until it ends on the opposite side in a sitting room for the employees.

The structure is made of Eternit panels, cut to size by a carpenter, which draws geometric patterns in the space. The deep anthracite gray that dominates the structure acquires hues of color thanks to the intense red of the fabric used to upholster the seats and part of the walls of the zone that joins the waiting room.

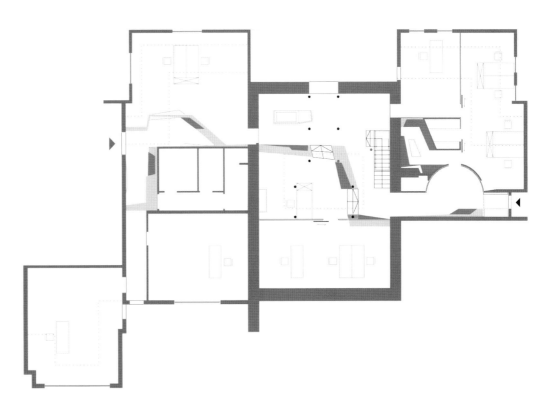

The waiting room of this office forms part of an
Eternit structure that performs other functions.

© Louise Melchior

N1 CREATIVE

BLACKSHEEP INTERIOR ARCHITECTURE & DESIGN

London, United Kingdom | 2005

Although small and compact, the wise distribution of colors and the delimitation of the surfaces of this lobby create a comfortable and visually attractive space, suitable for a communications consulting agency.

The internal scheme takes on the corporate colors that are white and ruby red. To compensate for the great luminosity of these shades and the flat walls, the counter of the reception and the back wall are covered with a grey glossy film. Over the same surface, a series of plasma screens transmit short films showing the graphic creations of the agency.

Suspended from the ceiling, a 4.9-foot-long curtain, complete with fine cords, limits the waiting area, while two white picket fences define the space destined for two basset hounds belonging to the owners, who, like their owners, show up at the office every day.

The glossy film that occupies the space under the picture window at the entrance is repeated in the interiors to create contrast with the corporate colors that dominate the lobby.

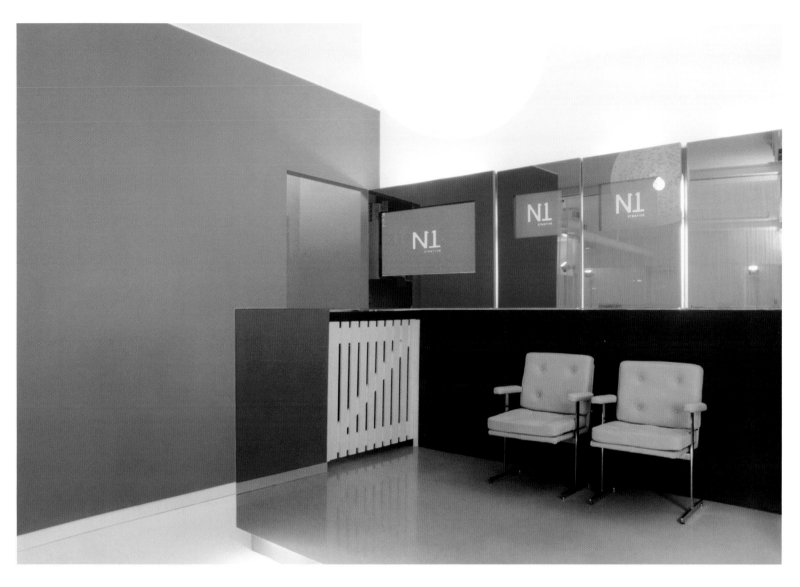

A mirror is created with a glossy film of sticky paper.

NEUSS PUBLIC UTILITIES OFFICES

EIKE BECKER ARCHITEKTEN

Neuss, Germany | 2007

The structure that protrudes from the entrance door of the new Public Administration building in Neuss creates a formal frame that repeats itself in the lobby. The inclined levels and the rectangular volumes are the main characters of this bereft space where one way leads to the offices and the other to the foyer that houses a cafeteria, a restaurant and a public information center.

The main counter is linked to the banister of the stairs that runs through three stories and ends in a skylight on the ceiling.

The predominating minimalist tone is reinforced by the colors; stark white on large surfaces and black on the borders of the rectangles throughout the stairs.

Pure minimalism, through net forms and the predominance of two colors.

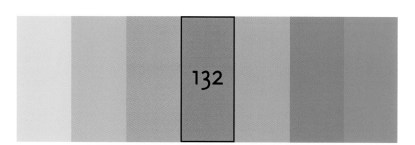

132

LEARN

Entrances to study and research centers that have been designed as places to meet and exchange knowledge.

© Eduard Heuber/Arch Photo, Tom Arban

GRAND JETÉ PROJECT

KPMB ARCHITECTS, GBCA ARCHITECTS

Toronto, Canada | 2005

Renowned as one of the most prestigious dance academies, the Canadian School of Ballet has embarked upon an expansion of its learning and training facilities. The new space for the "Grand Jeté" program has been designed as a vertical campus. Composed of three transparent bodies organized in the shape of a "U," the campus is organized around an edifice, built in 1856, known as the Northfield House.

The space between the old edifice and the new structures has been closed in order to create a lounge, which is the heart of the school. In this three-story-high structure, the old brick walls of the Northfield House coexist with a spacious steel oven in the shape of an "L" and a large digital screen where images are projected.

With the preservation of an existing historic building, the project, and in particular this space, establishes a model of harmonious co-existence of tradition with contemporary architecture.

The softly-shaped furniture creates spots of color
in this monochromatic space dominated by
glass, steel and stone.

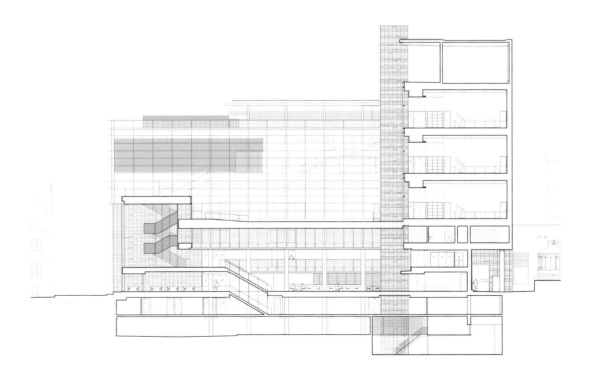

The new campus of the School of Ballet houses a central
space, which serves as access and meeting area.

ANTWERP UNIVERSITY

CREPAIN BINST ARCHITECTURE

Antwerp, Belgium | 2006

This building is characterized by conveying in its distribution an open and friendly atmosphere to the student. This institution is accessed through a grand central hall with a wide wooden-plated staircase, which has steps that can also be used as places to sit. From there, the auditoriums can be accessed.

The hall ceiling displays abstract drawings and written phrases in several languages that advocate in favor of coexistence. The work of art, carried out under the artistic direction of Michelangelo Pistoletto, called "Love Difference," represents the six Mediterranean seas. The light that emanates from large cylindrical voids illuminates the hall during the day and enhances the figures on the ceiling at night.

The spaces at lower heights, which are located in the back area, are presented in a design that is more consistent with the architecture of the area where the university is located: the historical Antwerp Quarter.

The steps of the spacious hall staircase are also
used as a sitting area.

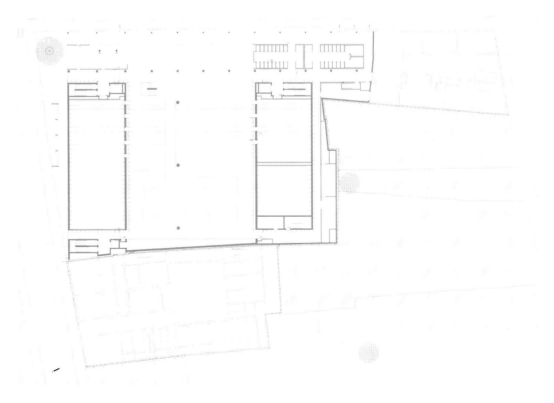

حب الاختلافات

Aimer les différences

The drawings on the ceiling represent the six seas: the Baltic, the Red, the Black, the Caribbean, the Mediterranean and the South China Sea, and make a plea to "Love Difference."

©Henning Larsen Architects

IT UNIVERSITY

HENNING LARSEN ARCHITECTS

Copenhagen, Denmark | 2004

In keeping with the character of a building which must establish a spatial dialogue with its surroundings, the design concept of this study center is that of a spatial network where each function remains in a tri-dimensional position around a panoptical display.

In the reception area, the hall offers a complete view of the University and from there, the study center appears as a dynamic structure where the activities all blend together on every level and whose common installations are at ground level.

The roof is a metallic net that allows natural light to enter and joins both sides of the building over the central patio. Composed of glass screens with different grades of opaqueness, the Eastern and Western façades reinforce the idea of a building open to the exterior. Some of the glass in the lateral walls contains engravings, while the others may be opened as part of the lateral ventilation system for the overall structure.

From the reception area, all the activity of the University can be viewed, thanks to the tri-dimensional composition of the building. The metallic net that extends over the hall and the lateral walls allow for the entrance of a great deal of natural light.

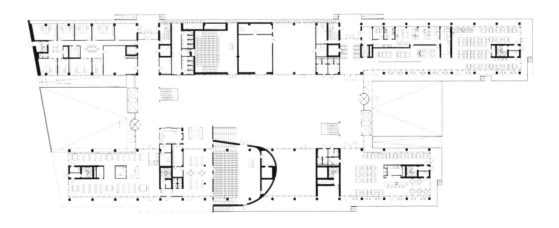

© Christian Richters

ABC FACULTY

ERICK VAN EGERAAT ASSOCIATED ARCHITECTS (EEA)

Utrecht, The Netherlands | 2005

The new building of the Biomedical Faculty (ABC) is part of the already existing Academic Hospital and is included within the master plan conceived more than ten years ago by the O.M.A. to modernize the University of Utrecht campus.

The building has two entrances: one that provides access to the faculty structure, leading directly to a spacious atrium where there is a student dining hall and the main stairway; the other connects with the university hospital.

The spacious faculty hall houses one of the three inside patios of cone-shaped glass that allow indirect sunlight to radiate to all corners of the building. These clear structures are the backbone as well as the atmospheric heart of the Faculty building.

Suspended in the center of the hall, a single and spectacular spider, designed by the celebrated artist Cerith Wyn Evans, highlights this space of vibrant colors and industrial aesthetics.

Through the use of intense and contrasting colors, such as red and green, the lobby acquires a contemporary and youthful air that matches the operations of the building.

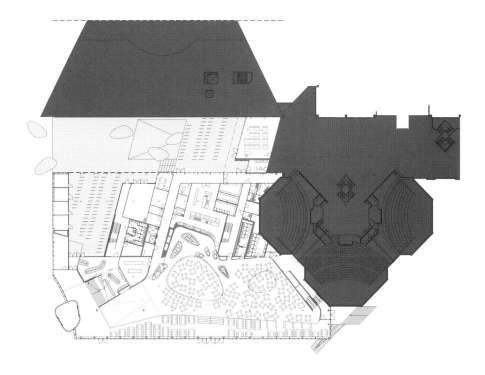

© Eduard Heuber/Arch Photo, Marc Cramer, Tom Arban/Tom Arban Photography

THE QUARTIER CONCORDIA

KPMB ARCHITECTS

Montreal, Canada | 2007

The Quartier Concordia is a complex of three buildings that houses the faculties of Engineering, Arts, and Business, widely interconnected in terms of technology and people.

Each building is organized on three levels. The intermediate structure contains multiple floors interconnected by stairs that open to a wide-ranging atrium. To emphasize this interaction, several sitting rooms are stationed around this central area. From the Art Faculty there are fantastic views of Montreal, while the main lobby of the Engineering Faculty contains stairs, which lead directly to the subway station located underneath the building.

In spite of having been conceived as a central traffic area, in this lobby you may breathe a breath of fresh air thanks to the lowered ceilings, the connections with the street, and the benches that invite people to slow down their pace and to gather round.

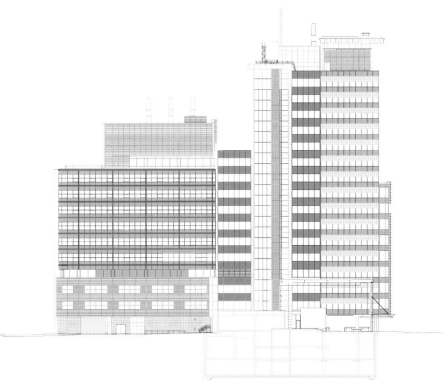

The faculties open to a central atrium, which is
surrounded by several lounges.

From the buildings there is access to a subway station situated
on the lower level.

© Adam Mørk

ALSION

KIM HERFORTH NIELSEN, BO BOJE LARSEN, KIM CHRISTIANSEN/3XN

Sønderborg, Denmark | 2007

This building complex houses culture, education and private research companies, which is why one of the main-planned objectives when the overall structure was designed was to allow for meeting places to facilitate the exchange of knowledge between students and scientists.

In consideration of the small scale of the city of Sønderborg, the architects decided to divide the large complex into a series of horizontally designed structures, with alternating atriums.

The ground floor of the building where the atrium is situated is presented as an open space, which outside of the normal working hours offers a wide variety of cultural events for the community. Additionally, it now serves as the new home for the city's Symphony Orchestra.

The glass walls and ceiling ensure the constant entry of natural light as well as a closely integrated connection with the surroundings.

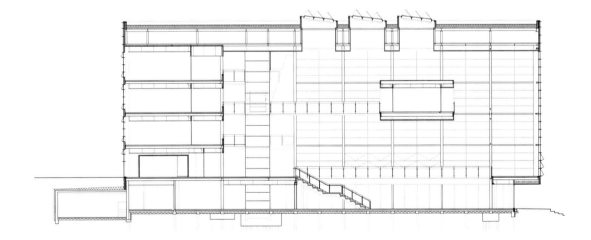

The wooden floors and the trees inside the atrium have transformed this space into an open plaza for the community.

© Thomas Mayer

PHÆNO SCIENCE CENTER

ZAHA HADID ARCHITECTS

Wolfsburg, Germany | 2005

This Science Center, the first of its kind in Germany, was erected as a mysterious object that stimulates curiosity and the drive to discovery. Its futuristic design, whose shapes make it similar to a space shuttle, include craters, terraces, plateaus and underground caverns.

The base structure is composed of two large cone-shaped elements. In addition to defining the main entrance and housing zones for service and diffusion, these cement "legs" operate as a supporting structure for the 26¼-foot-tall structure that emerges from the ground up.

From the lobby with inclined planes and irregular shapes, a large mechanical stairwell leads to the upper floors, where a panoramic view of the landscape of the city is offered, thanks to the large openings that seem to stretch out over the surfaces.

The lobby is situated on one of the "feet" over which the main body of the building is upheld.

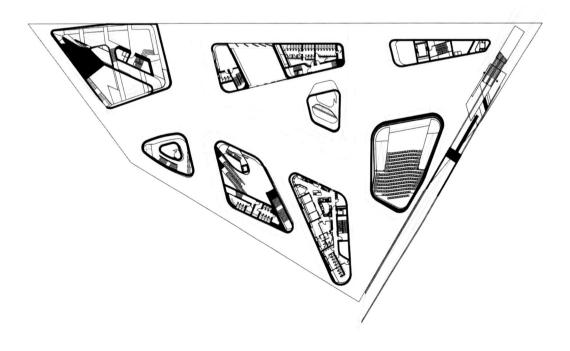

A magnificent mechanical stairwell offers
splendid views while it carries visitors to the
main level.

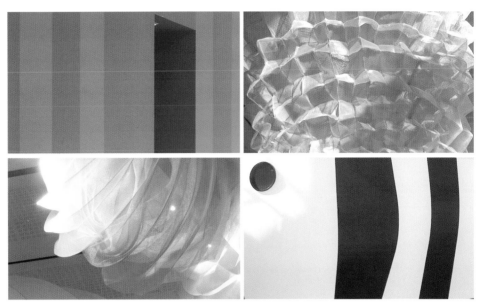

MEDICAL SCHOOL

ALSOP DESIGN

London, United Kingdom | 2005

Conceived as the working environment for 400 scientists, the astounding shapes and the vibrant colors generate an unexpected space for a first-class research center. The building has two different structures, connected by a bridge. The connection is also the access door to the main glass pavilion where some floating cameras of irregular shapes and intense colors remain suspended above the laboratory.

Each one of these compartments has been baptized with a name according to its shape. The "Mushroom Pod," is a structure that is open on top, which connects directly with the bridge and welcomes visitors, offering them a spectacular view of the installations.

The variable height of the encircling balustrade offers different degrees of privacy, since this space is also conceived as a place where meetings are held. In the center of the cabin a helical-coiled stairwell provides direct access to the laboratory, which is situated on the ground floor.

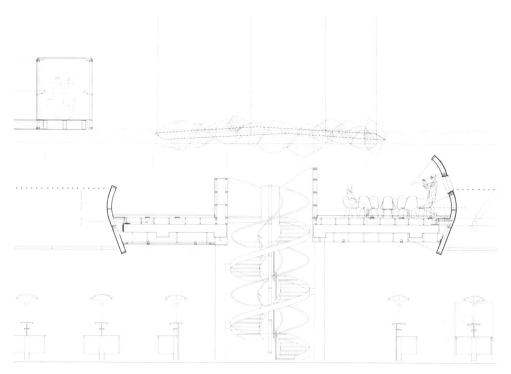

The cabin called "Mushroom Pod" welcomes
visitors that arrive at the medical laboratory.
The balustrade varies in height according to the
function assigned to the space, which may also
accommodate a small area for seminars.

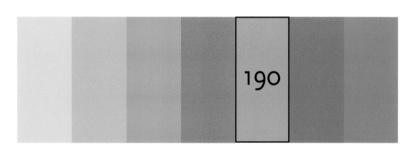

SHOW

The entrance areas to exhibition centers, fairs, special events, and temporary
facilities were created for impact.

© Coop Himmelb(l)au

AKRON ART MUSEUM

COOP HIMMELB(L)AU

Ohio, United States | 2007

The hall of this museum is shaped by "The Crystal," one of the three bodies in which the building is divided. The "Gallery Box" and the "Roof Cloud" are at the main entrance. The great dimensions and open character make it a flexible space that is suitable for banquets, art festivals, or presentations. This reinforces the concept of the contemporary museum as a place for exhibits as well as an urban meeting place for different collective manifestations.

Thanks to the volume and structure of "The Crystal" the air conditioning requires very little artificial energy. On the one hand, because the air conditioning is aimed at specific areas, where people are expected to be, and on the other hand, the tiles of the floor are equipped with water pipes that radiate heat or cold as needed and help maintain temperatures for longer periods of time.

The foyer of the museum was conceived as a space for banquets, presentations and art festivals.

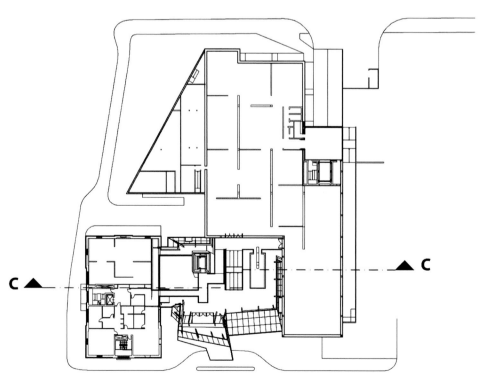

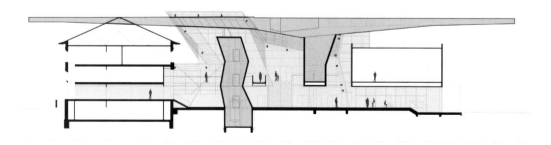

© Moreno Maggi

MILAN FAIR

MASSIMILIANO FUKSAS

Milan, Italy | 2005

The huge glass dome, extending at the top like a whirlpool, marks the entrance to the new Milan Fair, one of the largest buildings in Europe. From this spacious hall, 10,760,000 square foot built surfaces are accessed, which are located in the outskirts of the city.

The building extends over a lengthy axis covered by an undulating glass roof that differentiates all the spaces. This translucent blanket with a metallic skeleton adopts the forms of whirlwinds that sometimes sink in within the building and touch the ground, and other times rise up as if they were trying to touch the sky. The lobby brings together both "phenomena" and allows a glance as a foretaste of what awaits the visitor at the rest of the impressive premises.

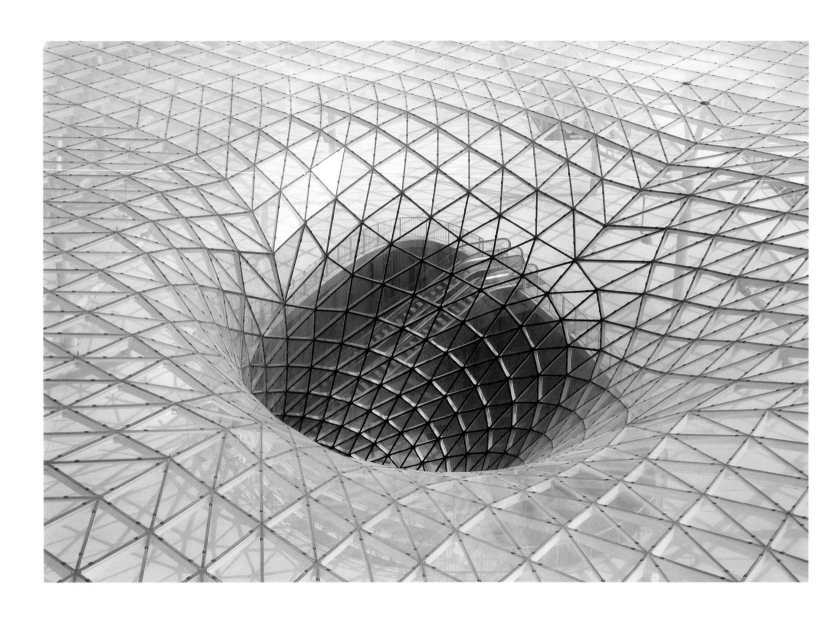

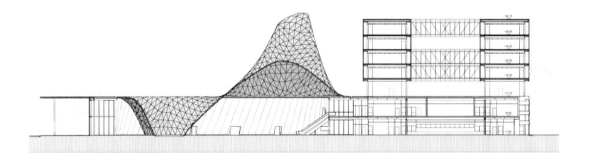

The crystal clear ceiling that runs through the
fairgrounds reaches one of its highest points at
the lobby.

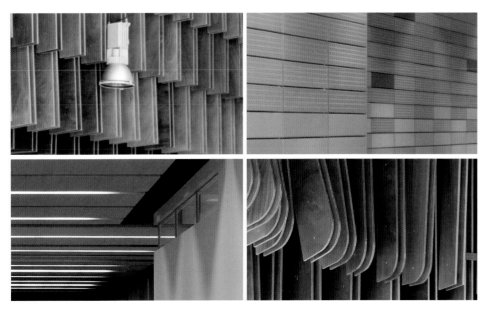

© Pedro Pegenaute

CONFERENCE AND EXHIBITIONS HALL

ARTEKS ARQUITECTURA, ESTER PASCAL

Ordino, Andorra | 2005

In the midst of the Pyrenees' idyllic landscape, this convention center is built with extensive spaces for exhibition and multi-purpose rooms. The entry hall, that also hosts the cafeteria, the reception and the cloakroom, has a distinct flair from the rest of the environments through the false pierced ceiling, which is built with sheets of wood.

The powerful expression of the composition is sustained by a complex geometry, which is displayed in the convergence of sheets in the reception area. Thanks to this structure, the space acquires a sense of warmth, not only because of the predominance of wood, but also because visually the space is not as high as the rest of the room.

In the entrance wall, stone has been used as interior lining, a pattern that repeats itself in other rooms within the building where materials that are part of the façades have also been used.

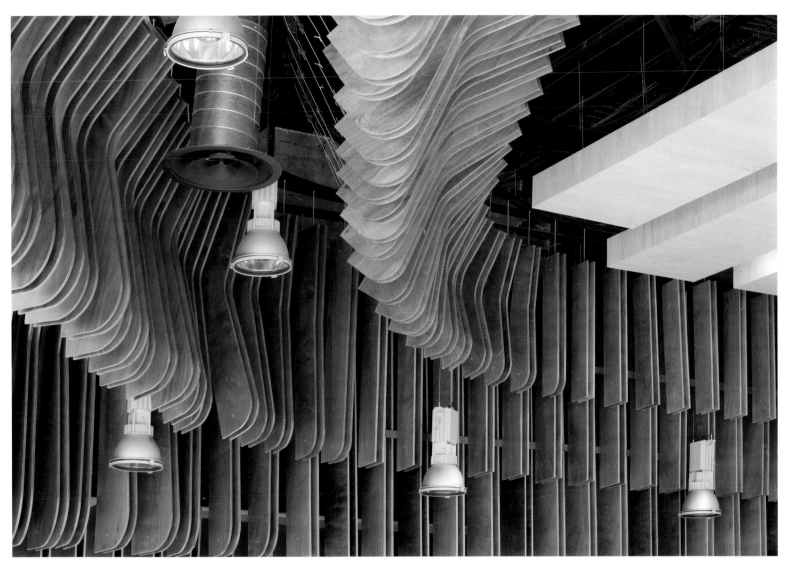

Complex geometry generates great visual impact that transmits a sensation of harmony.

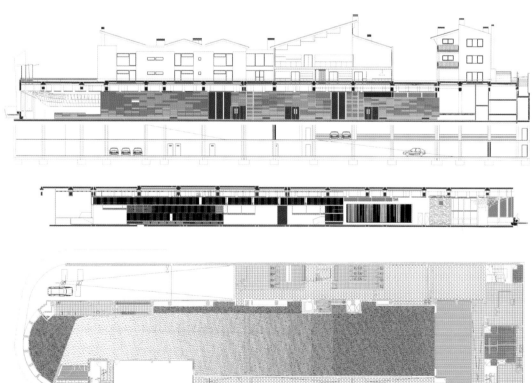

The lobby differs from the main exhibit room because of its false-pierced ceiling built with sheets of wood.

© Marc Gerritsen

BRIDGE UP TO ZENITH

EHS INTERNATIONAL

Taipei, Taiwan | 2006

Located in the new Bangiao district, this lobby belongs to the promotional building of a residential complex built by Continental Engineering Corporation. The reception, lobby, and hallway are all part of an area that is adjacent to the main street.

The entrance and gathering areas have been designed as a glass pavilion surrounded by water mirrors. The marble floor at the main lobby replicates within its natural pattern the flowing water effects of the surrounding ponds.

The main, zigzag-shaped stairway is located in the center of the building to separate the reception area from the private spaces that lead to the second floor. The ceiling allows the entrance of filtered natural light, creating an interesting effect on the stairway and main hallway.

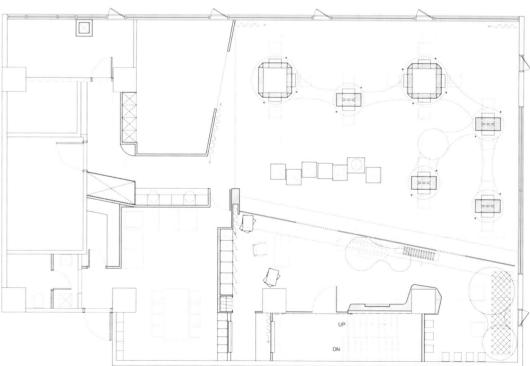

The combination of marble with water mirrors
transmits a relaxed and yet refined atmosphere.

© Marc Gerritsen

TREASURE BOX OF LIGHT

EHS INTERNATIONAL

Taichung, Taiwan | 2006

In contrast to the solid façade of this building, which seems to tower up from the ground as a powerful sculpture, the space inside this site, devoted to the exhibitions of properties, conveys a fluid and poetic atmosphere. The spacious two-story lobby is surrounded by a series of folding walls. The wall behind the reception counter is decorated with wood boards that are usually used on floors. Thus, it seeks to deconstruct the accepted perceptions about space planes inside an environment and consequently creates a spatial disorder.

A white marble staircase that leads the customer toward the meeting areas contrasts with the pitch black that is present in the rest of the surfaces. Just as the irregular openings in the building bring natural light inside, the mirrors embedded in the ceiling at various angles, reflect the urban landscape outside.

Angles that open at different degrees are a recurring feature in
the lobby, and configure science fiction scenarios.

The furniture and equipment define different
spaces within the same lobby.

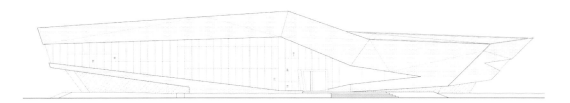

© Rimini Fiera-SIA Guest

THE LOVE HOTEL

STUDIO 63 ARCHITECTURE & DESIGN

Rimini, Italy | 2006

This hotel "boutique" project was presented at the November 2006, 56th edition of the SIA Guest Expo, in the international sector dedicated to hotel management. The proposal, which was specially built for the occasion, is a refined version of hotels whose rooms are rented by the hour.

From the lobby itself, the furniture of contemporary design moves away from the stereotype of this type of establishment and reinforces the idea of an open space where it is possible to live pleasant experiences. The quarters are laden with sensuality thanks to the intense red that tinges all surfaces. The space is intended to be the starting point for courtship which extends into the aisles, where verses of poetry that speak of love and passion are displayed in golden letters on the walls.

Between minimalism and sensuality, the lobby is a faithful
reflection of the concept of a hotel by the hour, which departs
from the vulgar stereotype.

© Luuk Kramer

VAN GOGH MUSEUM

CONCRETE ARCHITECTURAL ASSOCIATES

Amsterdam, The Netherlands | 2005

Within the framework of the Friday Nights show, the authorities of this classic museum in the Netherlands's capital aimed to find a design for the hall that would attract tourists and local citizens. According to the architects, "A museum is more appealing as a place where you can get a drink and meet new people." Therefore, they transformed the main hall into a temporary lobby with a large carpet and comfortable sofas.

Through the use of the blue color for all the elements, a "blue screen" effect was created. For example, if a Van Gogh painting is projected on the wall, the people who are in the lobby are filmed simultaneously; these people appear to be within the painting. This procedure, whose themes change according to the exhibitions, enable people to "walk" within the paintings and to experience art in a unique new way.

De scheppingskracht kan men niet inhouden, het moet er uit wat men voelt.

The creative power cannot be repressed, one must give vent to what one feels.

Vincent aan Theo, juni 1882 · Vincent to Theo, June 1882

De weg om te slagen is: moed houden en geduld en stevig doorwerken.

The way to succeed is to keep one's courage and patience, and to work on energetically.

Vincent aan Theo, februari 1886 · Vincent to Theo, February 1886

For Friday night events, the aim is to portray the museum as a relaxing gathering place.

The blue color of the carpet and sofas is meant to create a "blue screen" effect when the projections take place, thus the public seems to be an integral part of the paintings.

© Stockholm Furniture Fair

STOCKHOLM FURNITURE FAIR

KONSTANTIN GRCIC INDUSTRIAL DESIGN

Stockholm, Switzerland | 2007

Unlike the traditionally cold and stripped-down lobbies at exhibition centers, at this latest edition of the Stockholm Furniture Fair the reception area conceived by the German designer Konstantin Grcic displayed a cozy welcoming garden.

Through the use of plants, nets, and a surprising mixture of objects and furnishings, Grcic created a true oasis. The space presents some of the designer's most famous objects, such as the "Mayday" lamps made by the Flos Company, which belong to the permanent collection of the Museum of Modern Art (MoMA) in New York. Dozens of red umbrellas suspended from the ceiling add a touch of the cinematic, Mary Poppins style.

In previous editions, the designs of the entrance hall have been awarded to various professionals, such as the Spanish designer Patricia Urquiola, the French Ronan and Erwan Bouroullec and the Japanese Naoto Fukasawa.

The artificial garden in the lobby of the fair presents a surprising mixture of objects and furnishings designed by Konstantin Grcic.

PAMPER

Waiting rooms that define the first step toward the cult of beauty,
health and well-being.

BATHHOUSE SPA

RICHARDSON SADEKI

Las Vegas, United States | 2004

The Bathhouse spa is conceived as a pause from the bustling noise and stimulating world of Las Vegas, where this spa is located. The structure of this well-being center is inspired by the traditional Roman baths, but, unlike those, here the visitors are pampered by treatments in an exclusive environment, where privacy and serenity are the most cherished values.

Consistent with this spirit, the rooms are refined and present minimalist decor framed by spaces that are lined in black stone. The lobby is a bereft space where a row of benches stands out as an integral part of a sand-colored structure that is affixed to one of the walls.

From a few of the openings built into the wall, red color illumination highlights the slate black surfaces, generating an attractive contrasting decor that is replicated in the area of access to the elevator.

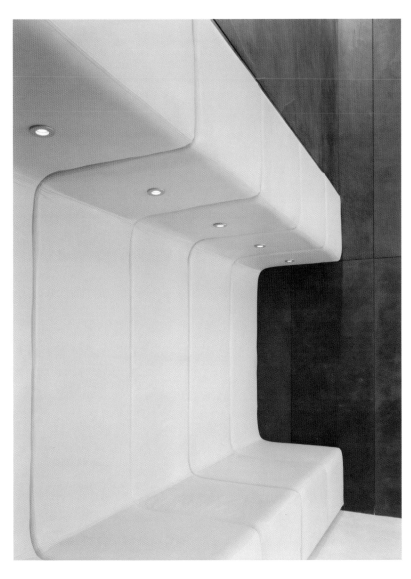

White leather seats cover part of one of the main entrance's walls.

The bereft surfaces of the lobby provide the atmosphere of privacy that was sought by this spa, which provides an oasis of serenity from the bustling noise of Las Vegas.

QANTAS FIRST-CLASS LOUNGE

MARC NEWSON, SÉBASTIEN SEGERS

Sydney, Australia | 2007

Designed by famous industrial designer Marc Newson, the Qantas first-class lounge at Sydney international airport boasts deluxe features. The lounge includes huge American oak sculptures that separate the space into defined areas. First- class passengers can unwind at a Payot Paris day spa, dine at a 48-seat open kitchen-restaurant with menus created by Australian chef Neil Perry, or relax in a quiet library decked with brown tiled floors and stocked with a selection of newspapers, magazines, novels, picture books and board games, which are stored in bright red cupboard/dividers. Other amenities include chair-side waiter service throughout the lounge, a dedicated entertainment area with banks of plasma screens, Sony Playstation 3 and Playstation Portable entertainment systems, and state-of-the-art business facilities with 11 PC workstations and complimentary wireless internet access.

The vertical garden designed by botanist Patrick Blanc, featuring over 8,400 individual plants and the specially composed music, complement this unique atmosphere, where waiting is no longer equivalent to wasting time.

The aeronautically-inspired base building provides customers
with an abundance of natural light and 180° panoramic views.

The furniture and luxurious finishes include leather lounge
chairs, recliners, and sofas by Italy's Poltrona Frau, dining
chairs and tables by Cappellini, Tai Ping wool carpets from
Hong Kong, Carrara marble and quartzite from
Switzerland.

© Jordi Miralles

NART DENTAL CLINIC

WORTMANN & BAÑARES ARQUITECTOS

Barcelona, Spain | 2007

This lobby transcends the architectural facts and is enriched by integrating sound, moving pictures, landscaping and fragrances around the concept of water as a different form of expressing purity and health at a dental clinic.

The space layout establishes three ramps, one to access the waiting room, another that leads to the reception area, and a third that gives access to the dentists' offices. The synthetic parquet planks used as wall coverings bring a sense of warmth, contrasting with the matte glass partitions that are illuminated by LED lights.

The furnishings are a far cry from an antiseptic and cold room. In order to achieve the best frame of mind in patients regarding treatments, a small bamboo interior garden has been conditioned to be seen from the resting area that is composed of "par joquer" sofas, and white puff chairs placed in the center of the room, which have been designed by the architects themselves.

Water in this setting, is the inspiring element: from the sculpture of a wave at the entrance, to the environmental music, and the video images, as well as the predominant fragrance within the compound.

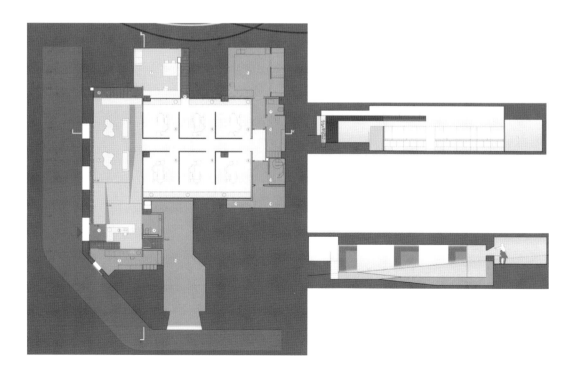

Parquet on the walls and glass partitions frame the access levels to the waiting room and to the clinic.

CARRAMASCHI CLINIC

ISAY WEINFELD

São Paulo, Brazil | 2005

A corridor unites the reception and the waiting room of this plastic surgery clinic, and occupies its center, where, thanks to the selected colors and almost minimalist aesthetics, a singular peacefulness floats in the air.

Absolutely devoid of any furniture, the entrance hall is a sober space, dressed by linen curtains that run through all surfaces, including the top band on the framework of the large opening that leads to the corridor. There, two thick layers of glass compose the door with fabric between both plates, creating a frosted glass effect that protects the privacy of patients.

A corridor, whose brightness is produced by the polished cement walls and the marble-like flooring, communicates with the waiting room, where chairs, sofas and coffee tables define a relaxed and cozy atmosphere.

The colors and materials create the intimacy and peacefulness that is necessary for this plastic surgery clinic.

Curtains that run across all the walls are the sole and powerful decorative element in the clinic's reception area.

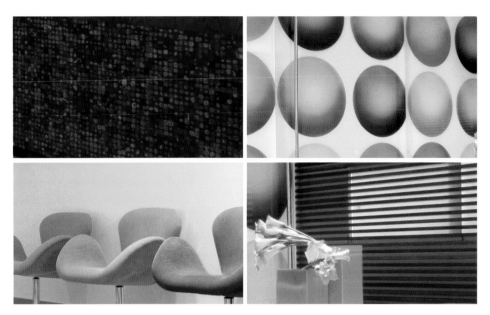

© Marcio Fragoso

MEDICAL CENTER

BRUNETE FRACCAROLI
ARQUITETURA E INTERIORES

São Paulo, Brazil | 2005

This medical clinic, where five pediatricians work, has a waiting room that is appropriate for keeping children entertained while waiting their turn to see the doctor. The interior design has been conceptualized to create an entertaining atmosphere to relax the small patients. The aim is to generate a friendly attitude toward the doctors, whose presence generally makes children fearful.

In the corridor that connects the waiting room with the clinics, a long magazine shelf keeps the traditional publications in an orderly manner. On the other hand, ergonomically-shaped and strikingly colorful armchairs are placed around a low table, and have their replicas in the circumference of the wall. The predominant pattern at the facility's reception area, it is also present in the plastic wall coverings for the crystal glass walls at the clinic.

Strikingly colorful armchairs aim to create a friendly
atmosphere for the children who come to this pediatric clinic.

The plastic wallpaper with big colored circles covers the clinic's main entrance wall.

1. Reception
2. Waiting room
3. Pantry
4. Room 1
5. Room 2
6. Room of manipulation and examination
7. Bathroom
8. Room 3
9. Room secretary

© Marc Gerritsen

NEO YES! HAIR SALON

ATELIER MARAIS DESIGN

Taipei, Taiwan | 2006

As a space intimately linked to creativity, fashion and design, this beauty salon is not just a place to get a haircut, but a center specialized in the latest trends.

Circumscribed within the trend known as the eclectic-chic look, the interior design brings together furniture and decorative details from a sophisticated neo-baroque style to rustic handmade crafts.

The reception area and the two waiting rooms are separated from the work area by a translucent crystal glass wall, which has engravings of flower silhouettes. In addition to having the typical elements of these kind of establishments, such as an area for magazines, television and product displays, this waiting room transforms during the weekend into a setting for live music concerts, managed by a DJ.

The waiting room is fashioned by two spaces that on weekends are the setting for performances by a DJ.

Eclectic chic: A Louis Ghost chair by Philippe Starck harmoniously coexists with a printed desk on the wall and rustic wood boxes in the background.

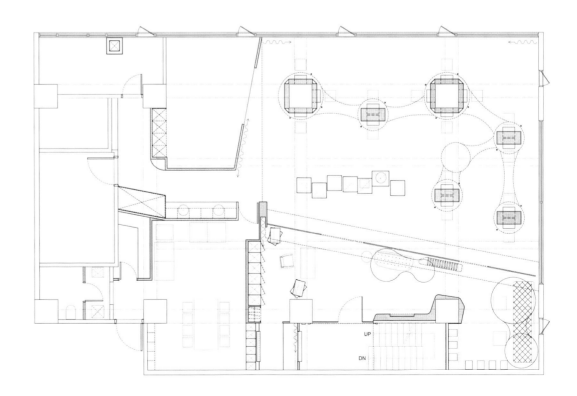

270

LIVE

Lobbies and waiting rooms from hotels and private homes where the conjunction
of art and fantasy remit exclusive habitats.

73 SPRING STREET

JEFFREY MCKEAN

New York, United States | 2005

The lobby of this building, situated in the midst of New York's Soho, utilizes textured cedar wood as a linear covering throughout the length of the main wall. The warmth of this natural material serves as a visual counterpoint to the iron structures and the stone fronts that characterize the buildings in the neighborhood.

The two volumes that project horizontally from the main wall and that serve as table and chair, seem to float over the state floor. The selection of this dark stone emphasizes the clarity of the cedar surfaces. Besides the lighting appliqués over the central volume, a hidden inlet in the ceiling lights the wall from above, creating a subtle playing of lights and shadows throughout the textured surface.

The cedar wood covering applied in a linear form, stands out as it contrasts with the slate floor and reinforces the sensation of warmth in the atmosphere.

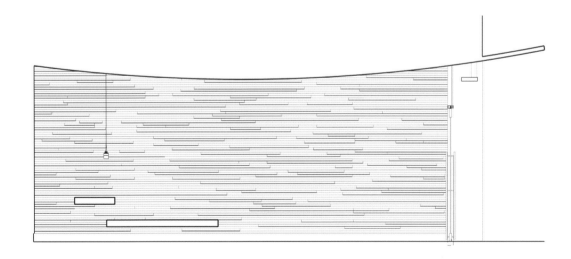

© Law Ling Kit, Virginia Lung

RESIDENTIAL LOBBY IN SHENZHEN

ONE PLUS PARTNERSHIP

Shenzhen, China | 2007

This lobby, belonging to an apartment building, is inspired by Chinese culture. In this frame, the bamboo plant, present in the majority of the architectural manifestations of the country, has been selected as the spinal cord for the design of this space.

Bamboo is a metaphor for strength and flexibility. It is the theme of many songs, poems, and paintings since the beginning of time, as well as a household item in the traditional agricultural sector.

Its linear shape inspires the design of this residential lobby, where the color green predominates and is intensified by special lighting. On the circular section, two central elements have been created for the residents' daily enjoyment; the fan-shaped mailboxes and a glass sculpture simulating a labyrinth.

The fan-shape of the residents' mailboxes is in itself a
sculptural element.

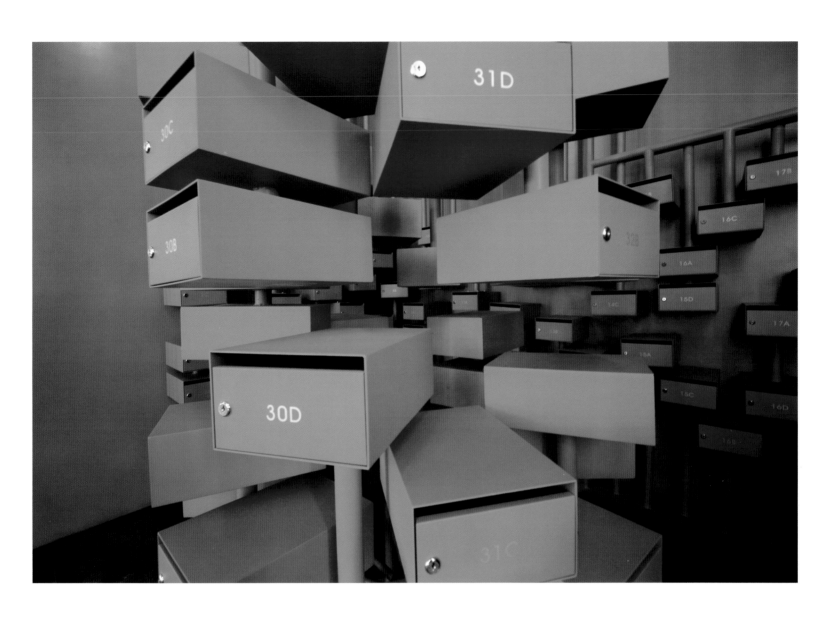

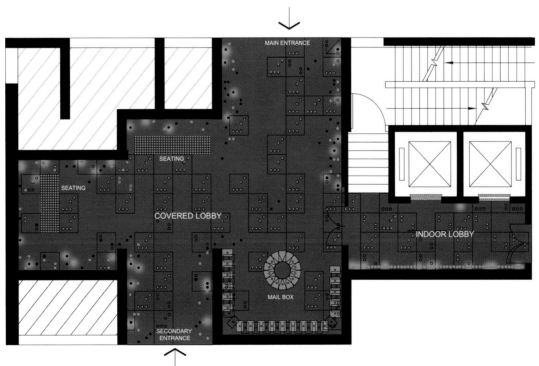

Bamboo, with its linear and flexible characteristics, inspires the design of this lobby.

WATER BALLET RESIDENTIAL DEVELOPMENT

MARK LINTOTT DESIGN

Taipei, Taiwan | 2006

The design of the lobby in this residential complex was inspired mainly by the forms of the movement of water. From the entrance, four metal figures stand out that appear to float over a tranquil tank. Each one represents a position taken from ballet. The pool reflects the figures, which makes them look as if they were moving.

The flashes and reflections are also due to the bright coverings of the ceiling and to the spider situated in the center of the lobby and made up of eight sets. There are a total of 960 spheres of glass that look like bubbles floating in the space.

On the back wall facing the entrance stands a golden metallic sculpture in the form of a tree, whose glass leaves sparkle as they move with the air.

Beyond the reception area, there is a more intimate lounge, furnished with pieces especially designed for this space through which a garden is accessed that leads to the residences.

About 960 crystal spheres make up the spider lamp situated
in the center of the lobby.

Each one of the metal figures at the entrance represents a
classic ballet posture.

About 960 crystal spheres make up the spider lamp situated
in the center of the lobby.

The proportions of the lobby are big but not
enormous, so as to maintain a human measure
in this residential building.

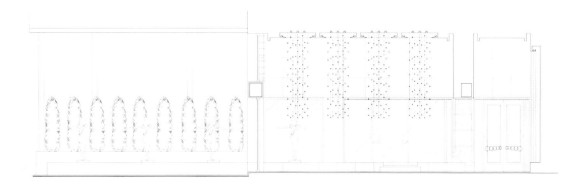

Each one of the metal figures at the entrance represents a
classic ballet posture.

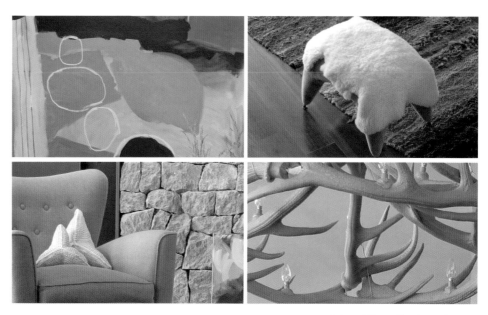

© Juan Hitters/Sur Press Agency

ESPLENDOR DE CALAFATE HOTEL

PLAN ARQUITECTURA

Santa Cruz, Argentina | 2005

Situated near the "End of the World," in the glacier region of the south of Argentina, this hotel presents a cozy lobby where the use of noble and typical materials from the region have not been an obstacle in imprinting a contemporary look on Patagonia.

The rugs are hand-woven wool from cow leather, and the molar-shaped stools designed by the architects themselves are covered with white sheepskin. The lamps are resin replicas of deer antlers, a common decorating recourse of the area.

One of the main attractions of this space is the main table made of red quebracho on top of which there are puzzles, mind-skill games and reading and writing materials.

The double fireplace is one of the pieces that lends character to the lobby. Made with black iron plates and detailed in structural steel, this, together with the stone, offers warmth to the waiting room.

Cushions made by Tramando decorate the seat with corduroy upholstering.

The big table, designed by the architects themselves, is made of "quebracho" wood.

The tapestry that hangs on the wall is the work of the Marosa
Group (Miguel Ronsino and Cecilia Timossi) and is inspired
by the Patagonic ice and skies.

The "turtle" stones that cover the walls come from quarries
adjacent to the lakes of the region.

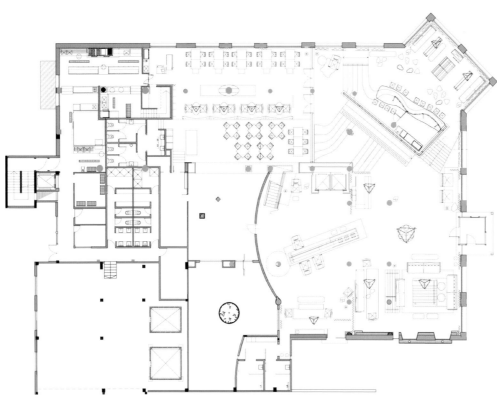

THE COVE ATLANTIS RESORT

JEFFREY BEERS INTERNATIONAL

Paradise Islands, Bahamas | 2007

Designed to create a fluid harmony between nature and architecture, the lobby of the hotel, The Cove, can well be described as a temple. Under the tall wood ceilings, a hall of stone columns decorated with cylindrical bronze lamps rises. Each one of these structures has a niche that houses aluminum sculptures and tint the space with a majestic tone. The seats, of geometric shapes and made of travertine marble, present pools of water in the center, which changes colors throughout the day, following the cycle of the sun.

The counter at the reception area is of mosaic and rosewood with mother-of-pearl inlays. The rugs are a granite and gold color to bring in the outside foliage. One of the focal points is the waterfall and a glass box filled with orchid petals that provide another touch of nature.

The access ways and internal pathways of the lobby have been designed so that visitors can enjoy the magnificent views of the beach and the Atlantic Ocean.

In the relaxing area, enormous leather sofas and ottoman chairs that range in color from gold to chocolate are combined with silk cushions.

A glass box table filled with orchid petals adds natural beauty to the space.

LA PURIFICADORA HOTEL

LEGORRETA & LEGORRETA

Puebla, Mexico | 2007

Before becoming a boutique hotel of evident colonial inspiration, this building was an ice factory that also purified and bottled water. Hence not only the name, but also the structure of the building registered as part of the historical heritage of the city, has maintained its essence.

The lower level of a great patio, partially covered by a roof, functions as a sitting room. The main stairwell that leads to the rooms acts as a sculptural element; it's part of the central fountain of the hotel and can be transformed into a stand for special events. As stated by the architects themselves, it is a modern interpretation of the exterior stairs found in all the homes of Puebla. In the same fashion, the traditional materials of the region, such as stones, cement tiles and stucco, coexist in this space with textures and shapes of contemporary design.

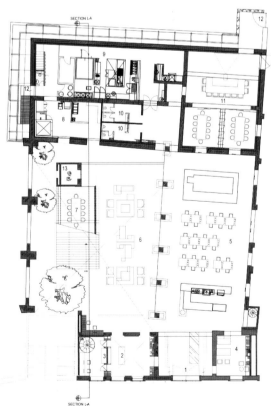

The stoves around which the vibrant-colored sofas are aligned, warm the nights, when temperatures drop to a few degrees above freezing.

DUOMO HOTEL

RON ARAD ASSOCIATES

Rimini, Italy | 2006

The front of this old building, located in the historic center of Rimini, announces the entrance to a vanguard space, linked by reflections, transparencies and dynamism. A great swaying door frames the entrance to the reception area, where the existing structure has been lined with the bronze skin that makes its way into the building. The focal point is the counter of the reception area, shaped by a spectacular ring of stainless steel, flamboyantly inclined and resting on a column. The back wall of this room is made of thin sheets of aluminum that allow daylight to come into the room, and glimpses of the offices located in the back.

The ultra-futuristic design of the lobby in this establishment from the Design Hotels chain emanates a vital atmosphere. The impact of the original installations, the intense colors and the risky shapes, establish a marked vanguard tone.

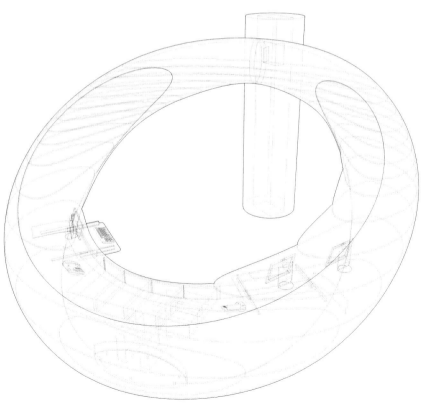

The shelves in the interior of the ring redefine the
horizontal topography of the counter.

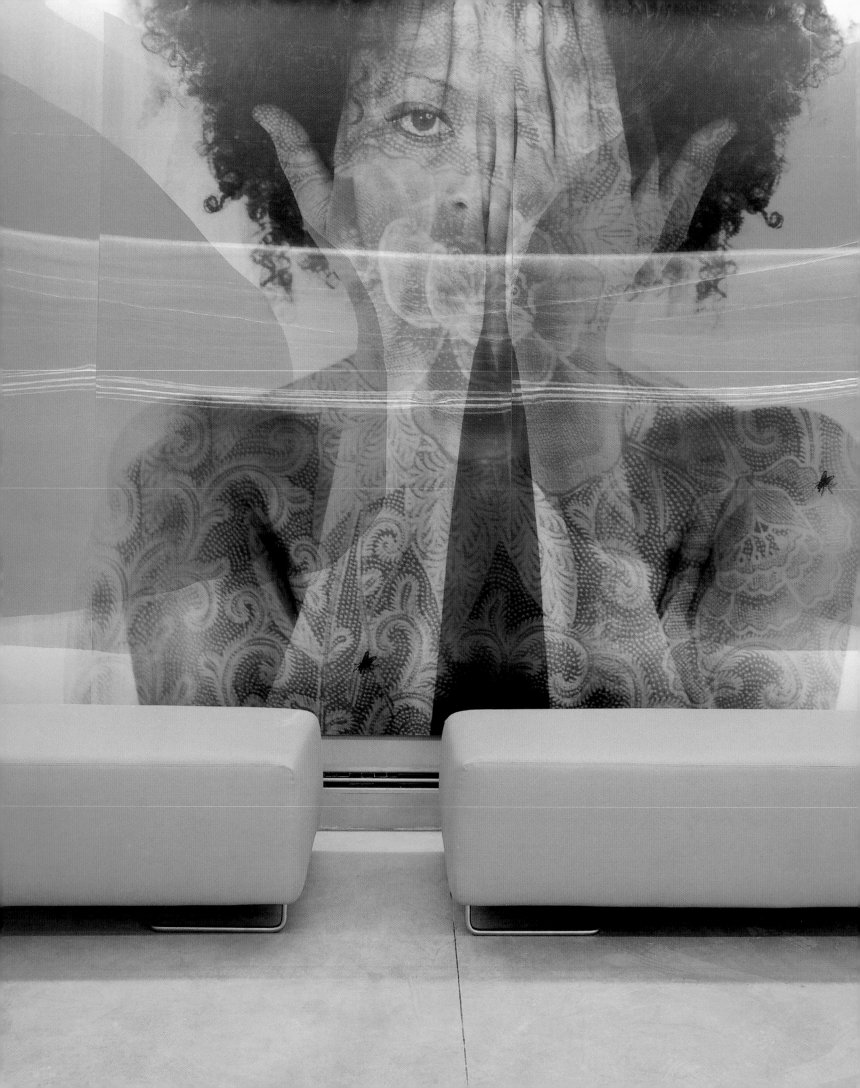

© Yael Pincus

MISS SIXTY HOTEL

STUDIO 63 ARCHITECTURE & DESIGN

Riccione, Italy | 2006

The Adriatic coast, between Rimini and Riccione, is the Mecca toward which the youth of Italy and Central Europe head every summer for their vacation. A product of the remodeling of a building in the 1950s, the new hotel from the clothing chain Miss Sixty fits in perfectly in the youthful context.

For the interior, thirty young artists have been summoned and they have created installations on the walls and mural paintings. The lobby is a sophisticated mix of modern and retro furniture, under the neo-baroque character of the wallpaper and the Murano chandeliers that are reflected in this composition of green and silver.

The reception counter, the bar and the stools were made of stainless steel. The walls and columns have been covered in wallpaper with velvet graphics over a mirrored background. Ottoman seats define the meeting and resting area as well as Tulip chairs placed in front of an impressive mural by Matteo Basile titled "Full of Grace."

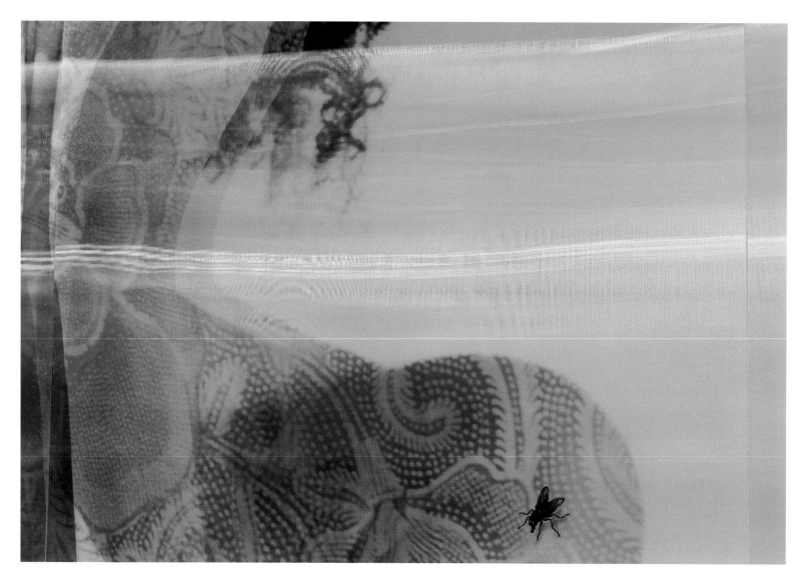

The Tulip chairs and ottoman seats situated in the waiting
room are from the Knoll Firm.

Each area of the hotel is dominated by a color. In the
lobby, green and silver define the youthful character of
the establishment.

NEW MAJESTIC HOTEL

DP ARCHITECTS, MINISTRY OF DESIGN, COLIN SEAH

Singapore, Singapore | 2006

After the renovation process that required the works of architects, designers and well-known artists, this old building, situated on one of the streets where wealthy men kept their mistresses, has become a majestic, youthful, provocative lady.

Framed in the style that the authors label as "patrimonial chic," the lobby shows the infinite creative possibilities that arise from the association of old and new. Like historic buildings, the structure of the ceiling is exposed and weathered by time. There might be those who think, upon entering the building, that the work is not completed.

The furniture, on the other hand, is comprised of collection pieces. Chairs, sofas, tables and lamps signed by the most famous designers of the XX century, define waiting areas around the winding stairs reminiscent of the old style of Miami Beach.

The original structure of the façade was preserved to contrast
with the hotel's interior contemporary design.

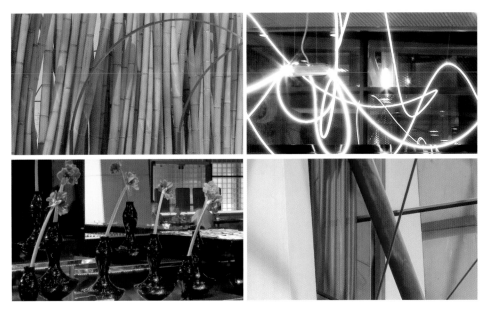

HESPERIA TOWER HOTEL

RICHARD ROGERS PARTNERSHIP & ALONSO BALAGUER Y ARQUITECTOS ASOCIADOS

Barcelona, Spain | 2006

The lobby of this particular hotel, converted into a transformation engine of its urban surroundings, is made of a lattice of enormous dimensions that joins the tower with another volume parallel to the street.

And so, the entrance to the hotel is shaped by an ample glass surface, which goes over the five lower floors and is held by means of an internal net of tensors and cables. This metal skeleton lightens the aluminum support structure and generates a space intimately united with the exterior.

Thanks to its great dimensions, the lobby houses two restaurants and two bars, each one with its own style. The spaces however, remain visually united, so that no matter where the eye roams, it will not miss the magnitude of the context.

The interior of the lobby is made in a way that all of its areas
remain visually connected.

The flexible neon lamp is model HLF from DAB and stands like a hanging sculpture in the center of one of the sitting areas of the lobby.

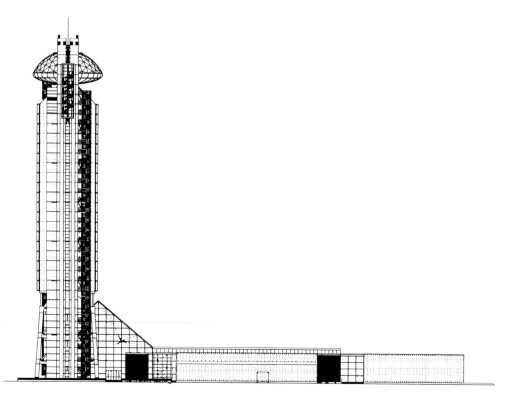

DIRECTORY

3XN A/S
Strandgade 73
Copenhagen 1401, Denmark
Tel: +45 7026 2648
webmaster@3xn.dk
www.3xn.dk

Alonso Balaguer y Arquitectos Asociados
Bac de Roda, 40
Barcelona 08019, Spain
Tel: +34 93 303 4160
estudi@alonsobalaguer.com
www.alonsobalaguer.com

Alsop Design Ltd
Parkgate Studio, 41 Parkgate Road
London SW11 4NP, United Kingdom
Tel: +44 20 7978 7878
Fax: +44 20 7978 7879
info@smcalsop.com
www.smcalsop.com

Arteks Arquitectura
L'Aigüeta 12 1r. pis,
Andorra La Vella AD50, Andorra
Tel: +376 823 202
info@arteks.ad
www.arteks.ad

Atelier Marais Design
First Floor, No. 32, alley 8, lane 36, section 5
East Road, Ming-Sheng
Taipei, Taiwan
Tel: +886 2 8787 4097
www.maraisdesign.com

Baldessari e Baldessari
Via Dante 17
38068 Rovereto, Trento, Italy
Tel: +39 0464 437777
info@baldessariebaldessari.it
www.baldessariebaldessari.it

Behnisch Architekten
163A Rotebühlstrasse
70197 Stuttgart, Germany
Tel: +49 711 607720
ba@behnisch.com
www.behnisch.com

Blacksheep Interior Architecture & Design
104-110 Goswell Road
London EC1V 7DH, United Kingdom
Tel: +44 20 7253 6393
contact@blacksheepweb.com
www.blacksheepweb.com

Brunete Fraccaroli Arquitetura e Interiores
Rua Guarará 261, 7º andar, Jardim Paulista
01425-00 São Paulo, Brazil
Tel: +11 3885 8309 / 3887 6834
brunete@osite.com.br
www.brunetefraccaroli.com.br

Carbondale Architects
54 Rue Etienne Marcel
Paris 75002, France
Tel: +33 01 44 82 76 76
info@carbondale.fr
www.carbondale.fr

Concrete Architectural Associates
Rozengracht 133 III
1016 LV, Amsterdam, The Netherlands
Tel: +31 20 5200 200
info@concreteamsterdam.nl
www.concreteamsterdam.nl

Coop Himmelb(l)au
2404 Wilshire Blvd., Suite No. 4K, 4th floor
Los Angeles, CA 90057, USA
Tel: +1 213 251 95 40
office@himmelblau-la.com
www.himmelblau-la.com

Crepain Binst Architecture
Vlaanderenstraat 6
B2000 Antwerp, Belgium
Tel: +32 3 213 61 61
mail@crepainbinst.be
www.crepainbinst.be

Despang Architekten
Am Graswege 5
30169 Hannover, Alemania
Tel: +49 511 882840
info@ despangarchitekten.de
www.despangarchitekten.de

DP Architects Pte Ltd
6 Raffles Blvd., #04-100 Marina Square
Singapore 039594, Singapore
Tel: +65 6338 3988
dparchitects@dpa.com.sg
www.dparchitects.com/main.html

EHS International Co
8A, No. 37, Jen-Ai Road, Section 4
Taipei, Taiwan
Tel: +886 2274 05158
ehs@ms31.hinet.net

Eike Becker Architekten
Kochstraße 22
10969 Berlin, Germany
Tel: +49 30 25 93 74 0
info@eb-a.de
www.eb-a.de

Erick van Egeraat Associated Architects (EEA)
Calandstraat 23
3016 CA Rotterdam, The Netherlands
Tel: +31 0 10 436 9686
eea.nl@eea-architects.com
www.eea-architects.com

Fletcher Priest Architects
Middlesex House
34/42 Cleveland Street
London W1T 4JE, United Kingdom
Tel: +44 20 7034 2200
enquiries@fletcherpriest.com
www.fletcherpriest.com

GBCA Architects
410 Adelaide St. West #500
Toronto, Ontario M5V 1S8, Canada
Tel: +1 416 929 6556
office@gbca.ca
www.gbca.ca

Gehry Partners LLC
12541 Beatrice Street
Los Angeles, CA 90066, USA
Tel: +1 310 482 3000
www.gehrypartners.com

Gudmundur Jonsson Arkitektkontor
Hegdehaugsveien 24
0352 Oslo, Norway
Tel: +47 23 20 23 50
gjonsson@online.no
www.internet.is/gudmundurjonsson

Henning Larsen Architects
Vesterbrogade 76
DK 1620 Copenhagen, Denmark
Tel: +45 82 333 000
info@henninglarsen.com
www.hlt.dk

Herault Arnod Architectes
123, Rue St Maur
75011 Paris, France
Tel: +33 1 48 07 81 40
zzz@herault-arnod.fr
www.herault-arnod.fr

Holodeck Architects
Friedrichstrasse 6
1010 Vienna, Austria
Tel: +43 1 524 81 33 0
vienna@holodeckarchitects.com
www.holodeckarchitects.com

Isay Weinfeld
Rua Andre Fernandes 175
Itaim-Bibi, 04536-020 São Paulo, Brazil
Tel: + 55 11 3079 7581
info@isayweinfeld.com
www.isayweinfeld.com

Jeffrey Beers International
156 5th Avenue 10th floor
New York, NY 10010, USA
Tel: +1 212 352 2020
info@jeffreybeers.com
www.jeffreybeers.com

Jeffrey Mckean
225 Broadway, 30th floor
New York, NY 10007, USA
Tel: +1 212 964 2300
info@jeffreymckean.com
www.jeffreymckean.com

Jestico & Whiles
1 Cobourg Street
London NW1 2HP, United Kingdom
Tel: +44 20 7380 0382
jw@jesticowhiles.com
www.jesticowhiles.com

Konstantin Grcic Industrial Design
Schillerstrasse 40
D-80336 Munich, Germany
Tel: +49 89 5507 9995
office@konstantin-grcic.com
www.konstantin-grcic.com

KPMB Architects
322 King Street West, 3rd floor
Toronto M5V 1J2, Canada
Tel: +416 977 5104
kpmb@kpmbarchitects.com
www.kpmbarchitects.com

Legorreta & Legorreta
Palacio de Versalles 285-A
Lomas de Reforma, México D.F. 11020, México
Tel: +52 55 52 51 96 98
info@lmasl.com.mx
www.legorretalegorreta.com

MAP Architects
Teodoro Roviralta 39
08022 Barcelona, Spain
Tel: +34 932 186 358
map@mateo-maparchitect.com
www.mateo-maparchitect.com

Marc Newson Ltd
175-185 Gray's Inn Road
London WC1X 8UP, United Kingdom
Tel: +44 207 287 9388
pod@marc-newson.com
www.marc-newson.com

Mark Lintott Design
418 Lane 101, Da-an Road, Section 1
Taipei, Taiwan
Tel: +886 2275 12 278
emld@ms1.hinet.net
www.mld-design.com

Massimiliano Fuksas
Piazza del Monte di Pietà 30
00186 Rome, Italy
Tel: +39 06 68807871
office@fuksas.it
www.fuksas.it

Ministry of Design
16B Trengganu St
Singapore 058470, Singapore
Tel: +65 62225780
studio@modonline.com
www.modonline.com

Neutelings Riedijk Architecten
P.O. Box 527
NL-3000 AM Rotterdam, The Netherlands
Tel: +31 10 404 66 77
info@neutelings-riedijk.com
www.neutelings-riedijk.com

Office for Metropolitan Architecture (OMA)
Heer Bokelweg 149
3032 AD Rotterdam, The Netherlands
Tel: +31 10243 82 00
office@oma.nl
www.oma.eu

OMM Design Workshop
94 Florida Road
Durban 4001, Southafrica
Tel: +31 3035191
admin@designworkshop.co.za

One Plus Partnership Limited
4/F, 332 Lockhart Road, Wanchai
Hong Kong
Tel: +852 2591 9308
admin@onepluspartnership.com
www.onepluspartnership.com

Peter Marino
150 East 58 Street
New York, NY 10022, USA
Tel: +1 212 752 5444
www.petermarinoarchitect.com

Plan Arquitectura
Godoy Cruz 1541
Buenos Aires, Argentina
Tel: +54 11 4775 7016
info@planarquitectura.com.ar
www.planarquitectura.com.ar

Richard Rogers Partnership
Thames Wharf, Rainville Road
London W6 9HA, United Kingdom
Tel: +44 (0) 20 7385 1235
www.richardrogers.co.uk

Richardson Sadeki
52 Walker Street, 4th floor
New York, NY 10013, USA
Tel: +212 966 0900
info@rsdnyc.com
www.rsdnyc.com

Ron Arad Associates
62 Chalk Farm Road
London NW1 8AN, United Kingdom
Tel: +44 20 7284 4963
info@ronarad.com
www.ronarad.com

Sébastien CG Segers Architecte DPLG
19 rue Béranger
75003 Paris, France
Tel: +33 6 8124 7414
studio@sebastiensegers.com
www.sebastiensegers.com

SMC Alsop
41 Parkgate Road
London, United Kingdom
SW11 4NP
Tel: +44 0207 978 7878
mail@smcalsop.com
www.alsoparchitects.com

Studio 63 Architecture & Design
Via Santo Spirito 6
50125 Florence, Italy
Tel: +39 055 2399 252
info@studio63.it
www.studio63.it

The Lawrence Group, New York
307 West 38th Street, Suite 1618
New York, NY 10018, USA
Tel: +1 212 764 2424
info@thelawrencegroup.com
www.thelawrencegroup.com

UN Studio
Stadhouderskade 113
P.O. Box 75381
1070 AJ, Amsterdam, The Netherlands
Tel: +31 20 570 20 40
info@unstudio.com
www.unstudio.com

Wortmann & Bañares Arquitectos
Muntaner, 341, 1.°
Barcelona 08021, Spain
Tel: +34 93 240 40 84
info@wb-arquitectos.com
www.wb-arquitectos.com

Zaha Hadid Architects
10 Bowling Green Lane
London EC1R 0BQ, UK
Tel: +44 20 7253 5147
mail@zaha-hadid.com
www.zaha-hadid.com